## MIGHTY MACHINES
# MONSTER TRUCKS

QEB

Quarto is the authority on a wide range of topics.

Quarto educates, entertains and enriches the lives of our readers—enthusiasts and lovers of hands-on living.

www.quartoknows.com

Scholastic Book Fairs – US
Written by Clive Gifford
Edited by Ellie Brough
Design by Starry Dog Books
Picture Research by Sarah Bell

First published in 2018 by QEB Publishing,
an imprint of The Quarto Group.
6 Orchard Road, Suite 100,
Lake Forest, CA 92630.
T: +1 949 380 7510
F: +1 949 380 7575
www.QuartoKnows.com

A CIP record for this book is available from the Library of Congress.

ISBN 978 1 91241 362 1
9 8 7 6 5 4 3 2 1
Manufactured in Guangdong, China TT042018

FSC
www.fsc.org
MIX
Paper from responsible sources
FSC® C016973

# CONTENTS

# What are MONSTER TRUCKS?

Monster trucks are built to thrill. These big, bright vehicles are fitted with big wheels and strong **engines**. Many race around dirt tracks in front of large crowds. Others perform amazing stunts such as jumps or crushing cars.

Tire

Men and women race monster trucks. This is Karen Shutler who drives Grim Reaper.

Everything about monster trucks is super-sized. Their tires, for example, can be as tall as a regular car! Most monster trucks weigh over four **tons**.

# Making a MONSTER

Monster trucks ride high on big wheels and chunky tires. A **suspension** system connects the wheels to the truck's body. It cushions the vehicle as it drives over bumps and lands after a jump.

Monster truck tires can measure 66 inches tall. They are not pumped up very much as this helps them create soft landings.

**Springs** help the wheels travel over bumps.

Many trucks have a see-through plastic floor in the **cab** so the driver can see where the truck will land when jumping.

A long rod called an **axle** joins each pair of wheels.

# Making it SAFE

Safety cage

Monster trucks are built around a sturdy frame. It is usually made of strong steel tubes all joined together. The truck's body panels are made of light **fiberglass** and are fitted to the frame.

**Steel frame** The part of the frame that surrounds the driver is called the **safety cage.** It protects the driver if the truck rolls over.

**Crash helmet protects head**

The plastic windshield protects the driver from dirt and objects flying toward their head.

**Driver strapped securely into their seat**

**Fire extinguisher**

# Monster RACERS

Monster truck races draw large crowds. Trucks can be raced in a stadium or over rough ground. Some races are held on beaches, while hill climbs see trucks speed up steep slopes.

**First past the finish line wins!**

**Trucks can reach speeds of over 60 miles per hour.**

Raminator reached a speed of 99.1 miles per hour in 2014. This makes it the fastest monster truck in the world.

Pairs of monster trucks compete against each other. They race side by side over identical **circuits**.

# BIGFOOT

Bob Chandler built one of the first-ever monster trucks in 1975. His friends nicknamed the truck Bigfoot. The name stuck and there have been 20 Bigfoot trucks since. These have entertained fans at hundreds of shows with their speed and stunts.

Bigfoot 1 was built from a Ford F250 **pickup truck** with big wheels and lots of lights added.

Bigfoot 21 first appeared in 2015 and won the very first race it entered!

**Bigfoot 21**

Bigfoot 5 is a real monster. It stands 15 feet, 6 inches tall. Its tires weigh 2,400 pounds each and are as tall as an African elephant!

# Looking
# THE PART

Monster trucks are decorated in bright, colorful designs. Some feature fun extra parts to make them look less like a truck and more like an animal.

Tailgator kicks up lots of dust. The front of its body is shaped like sharp alligator teeth.

**Bony frill like a dinosaur**

Jurassic Attack has a pointed nose and three horns just like a Triceratops dinosaur. It has been driven in competitions by three brothers: Kevin, Nathan, and Linsey Weenk.

# Leaping LEGENDS

Jumps were the first tricks that monster truck drivers mastered. The first jumps were just a few feet long, but now monster trucks are able to leap HUGE distances.

In 2013, Joe Sylvester made the biggest-ever leap in a monster truck. His Bad Habit truck jumped a record distance of 237½ feet. That's two and a half times the length of an NBA basketball court!

Bad Habit flies through the air

# Super stunts
# FLIPS & SPINS

At freestyle competitions monster trucks amaze fans with great tricks and stunts. The ultimate trick is to flip a truck over in the air, like a gymnast does a **somersault**.

Trucks can spin around and around really fast in a tight circle. This trick is called a **donut** and it sends big dust clouds into the air.

The truck and driver go upside down.

In 2015, Tom Meents, driving Maximum Destruction, did a double back flip. Wow! In 2017, Lee O'Donnell, driving Mad Scientist, performed the first monster truck front flip.

Trucks speed up a curved ramp to flip backward.

# Super stunts
# WHEELIES

**Wheelies** see trucks drive along on only two wheels. To perform this popular trick, the driver **accelerates** sharply. This makes the front of the truck rear up and its wheels rise into the air.

Nose wheelies are called **"stoppies."** The driver hits the truck's **brakes** sharply to send the back of the vehicle up into the air.

During a wheelie, some drivers will bounce their truck up and down on its rear tires. This trick is called a **"pogo."**

Rear tires grip the ground

# CRAZY trucks

All monster trucks look great but some look more unusual than others.

Hold the bus! Higher Education looks like a souped-up school ride. It is actually three quarters the size of a regular school bus.

**The truck's 18-foot-long sides are made of board and painted yellow.**

Red Dragon is Europe's only monster ride truck. Its frame is specially modified to carry up to ten passengers for a thrilling monster truck experience.

# TRACKED trucks

Meet the monster trucks that don't run on tires. Instead, they have long belts called **tracks** which are turned by many wheels. Tracks are also found on tanks and **bulldozers**.

Chevrolet pickup truck body

SCOTT MAY'S DAREDEVIL STUNT SHOW THUNDER

This hefty tracked truck is called Armour-Geddon. It crushes cars as if they were cardboard boxes! The truck's body can flip up so fans can see the driver.

Thundertrax started out as an army vehicle. Scott May found it rusting in a scrapyard and turned it into an exciting monster truck.

25

# PAINTED trucks

Monster trucks stand out from the crowd with their eye-catching body designs. Some are covered in printed stickers. Others are decorated with hand-painted works of art.

It was a big job decorating the Sin City Hustler. It is the longest monster truck in the world. The truck is 32 feet long and took 15 months to build.

The Monster Medic truck dazzled fans with its bright paint job when it first appeared in 2014. It has a one-eyed, green alien doctor on its body!

Seats inside for up to 12 passengers

# QUIZ and ACTIVITIES

Test your monster truck knowledge!

1. What sort of dinosaur does the Jurassic Attack monster truck look like?
a) Triceratops
b) Stegosaurus
c) Tyrannosaurus rex

2. Which monster truck reached a record speed of 99.1 miles per hour?
a) Avenger
b) Thundertrax
c) Raminator

3. Which truck holds the record for longest jump?
a) Bad Habit
b) Bigfoot 14
c) Avenger

4. How much does each of Bigfoot 5's tires weigh?
a) 120 pounds
b) 460 pounds
c) 2400 pounds

5. How many jet engines power the Shockwave truck?
a) 1
b) 3
c) 5

6. What trick is performed when a truck spins around and around on the same spot?
a) wheelie
b) flip
c) donut

8. Grab some pens and paper and draw your very own monster truck. Give your truck a fun name.

What colors and design will appear on its body?

Will you add extra parts onto its body?

Will you give it big tires or tank tracks?

Is your truck in a race, jumping off a ramp, or crushing cars?

9. Can you unscramble the letters to name three famous monster trucks?

a) tgoboif

b) rmroainrt

c) ranuhrxtted

10. Which route should the monster truck take to reach the dirt ramp?

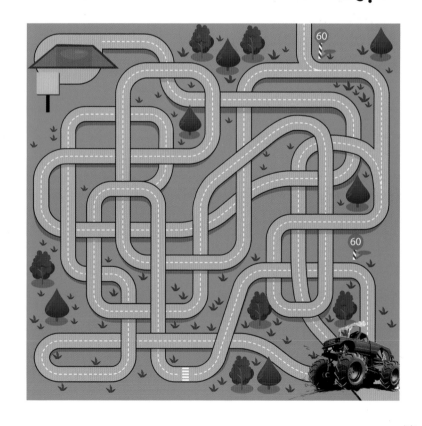

# GLOSSARY

**accelerate**
To speed up and go faster

**brakes**
Parts of a vehicle which slow it down

**bulldozer**
Heavy vehicle that runs on tracks with a large blade at the front used for pushing earth away

**cab**
Part of the truck where the driver sits and controls the vehicle

**circuit**
Track built for trucks to race on

**donuts**
Trick where a truck spins around and around on the same spot

**engine**
Part of the truck which generates the power to move it forward

**fiberglass**
Strong, light plastic material made stronger by fibers of glass running through it

**freestyle**
Part of a monster truck event where trucks perform tricks and stunts

**pickup truck**
A small truck with a cab and an open back, often used by farmers and builders

**pogo**
A trick where a truck driver does a wheelie and then bounces on the back tires

**safety cage**
Frame, often made of steel tubes, which protects a driver should their truck crash or roll over

**somersault**
An acrobatic trick where a person turns head over heels in the air and lands on their feet

**springs**
A metal coil which can be pushed and pulled but returns to its original shape

**stoppie**
A trick where the driver brakes suddenly to balance the truck on its front wheels only

**suspension**
Parts which connect the body and the wheels of a truck together. They help give it a smoother ride when running over bumpy surfaces.

**ton**
A heavy amount of weight equal to 2,000 pounds

**tracks**
Metal or rubber belts which run around wheels to help a vehicle cross rough ground

**wheelie**
Trick where a truck lifts its front wheels off the ground so it drives on one pair of wheels

# INDEX

**Picture credits**
(t=top, b=bottom, l=left, r=right, c=centre, fc=front cover, bc=back cover)

**Alamy**
fc Jack Sullivan/Alamy Stock Photo, 6/7 © Andrew Steven Graham/Alamy Stock Photo, 22 © Xinhua/Alamy Stock Photo/Vaters Motorsports, LLC. 1981-2018 © TM All Rights Reserved

**Bigfoot ©2005-2018 All rights reserved. Bigfoot 4x4, Inc. Bigfoot4x4.com**
4/5 © Gyln Thomas/LOOP Images (Getty), 6b & 21 © Jeff Luckey Photo, 8/9, 12b, 12/13, 18b, 29t, bcc & bcl © Maas Media, 9b © Michael Doolittle/Alamy Stock Photo, 10/11 © Michael Doolittle/Alamy Stock Photo/ Raminator – Hall Bros. Racing Inc, 13t © Ian Gadnall/Alamy Stock Photo

**Big Pete Ltd**
5t, 7t & 25t © Karen Shutler

**Danny Maass/ Maass Media**
1, 11t © Maass Media/Raminator – Hall Bros. Racing Inc, 19 © Maass Media/www.avengerracing.com, 20b © Maass Media/with permission by Dirt Crew www.detpowersports.com, 27t © Maass Media/Monster Medic monster truck

**Getty**
26/27 © Jen and Brad Campbell/Big Toyz Racing www.bigtoyzracing.com/ Getty Images

**Jeff Luckey**
14b © Jeff Luckey Photo/Tailgator Copyright Big Dawg 4x4 2000-2017, 16/17 © Jeff Luckey Photo/Courtesy of Bad Habit www.rigidindustries.com, Joe Sylvester and Columbus PA Cornfield 500

**Jurassic Attack**
15 © www.jurassicattack.com

**Red Dragon**
23t, bcr © Red Dragon Monster Ride Truck http://www.reddragonmonstertruck.com

**Shutterstock**
29b © Savgraf/Shutterstock, © Kirill Galkin/Shutterstock & © Mechanik/ Shutterstock, 28/29 © My Portfolio/Shutterstock

**Thundertraxx**
24/25 © With permission by Thundertrax

**We would also like to thank all the featured trademarks for their kind help and for granting us permission to feature their trucks in this book.**